THE SUN RISES AT MIDNIGHT

The Story of the Barrier Breaking Woman

Lisa Jackson

© 2018 Lisa Jackson
All rights reserved.

ISBN: 1981751084
ISBN 13: 9781981751082

DEDICATION

I dedicate this book first to my children and granddaughter. I love you all, and although times were tough and I didn't make the best choices the grace of God kept us. I pray that I showed you to never give up. And to trust in the Lord. To my loving Husband Jim, you came in like a thief in the night stealing my heart and Like a warrior protecting it. You have been patient with me during this process, the support you show daily I love you dearly baby, thank you for rocking with me. To my Mother Boo You are the reason I am here I love you and I want you to know beauty for ashes our story is restoration. To my Grandparent's Thank you for depositing into me roots of a palm tree not easily broken still standing type DNA. Gammie Thank You for everything for introducing me to my Savior for singing hymns in the night for praising Him with tears while driving from church for never being ashamed to say Thank you Jesus, for loving me the best way you knew how. And to my sisters and brothers I love you all more then you will ever know.

The mission of The Barrier Breaking Woman

I am a Barrier Breaking Woman. My name is Lisa Jackson and I wrote my story in hopes to positively impact. I have decided to dedicate my life to helping others by being more loving, empowering with truth, compassion, and building up instead of tearing you down. By God's power and grace, I will reach many of all backgrounds

Dear little soul the shame is not yours, and it never was. Speak out, don't be afraid God will protect you. He is our vindicator I didn't know that then, but I know it now.

> **"They have greatly oppressed me from my youth," let Israel say;**
> **But they have not gained the victory over me.**
> **Plowmen have plowed my back and made their furrows long.**
> **But the Lord is righteous;**
> **He has cut me free from the cords of the wicked.**
>
> **Psalm 129:1-4**

If you know of anyone who needs help getting out of a situation tell someone

ACKNOWLEDGEMENTS

I want to say Thank You Father God My Lord for developing me for keeping me for loving me when I know I was not easy to love for knowing the real me for your mercy and grace over my life for giving me a spirit of forgiveness and a desire to want to know you.

I also would like to thank all the people who God used to help me along the way too many to name but you know who you are I cherish the moments that God blessed me with you all Thank you for encouraging me for believing when I was in doubt for cheering even though I was sitting on the sidelines I love you all many blessings.

FOREWORD

In life we all go through some things, but some go through a bit more than others in different ways. While that is not to slight anyone reading this book, it's just to say that when you have been through hell and back and have made the decision to not only keep on going, but to forgive in the process - you are one heck of a person.

Lisa has proven that though life's experiences can knock you down, they can't keep you down unless you let them.

The Sun Rises At Midnight is the true story of a woman's decision to break the barriers that life's circumstances tried to impose on her and to reach out to others and help them break their own barriers as well.

Breaking barriers is not just about getting up when you are knocked down, it's about kicking the culprit in the teeth and continuing to move forward after doing so.

Lisa takes it a step further by reaching back to extend a hand to help others even in the midst of her own process.

The Sun Rises at Midnight will make you cry, laugh, and cheer not only for Lisa, but it will have you cheering for yourself and everyone who ever wanted to break barriers in their life but didn't think it was possible.

This book is a true page turner and Lisa is truly a "Barrier Breaking Woman" that proves that no obstacle is too big unless you allow it to be.

You should also know that before you finish reading this book, you will know that faith is real and God's Grace really is sufficient enough for us all.

Rosena E. Colquitt-Flynn
Author of Seasons of Change
Founder of Positivity Chronicles & Seasons of Change Bent But Not Broken

DIRTY RED

From the time I was very young, I was odd, different than all the kids in my family. I looked different, spoke different, hell I even smelled different. Dirty Red was the nickname, given to me by my Grandfather, on my mother's side. Why well I was this golden brownish-red little chubby girl with sandy brown hair and dark golden edges with highlights and my mom says remarkable green eyes, rare around these parts for a black kid. I was the oldest of my mother's kids, the middle of my cousins, and the youngest and only girl on my father's side. So where did I fit in? I was the kind of kid that drove her mother insane although I was not a bad child I gave many a run for their money. My mother tells me I was always very independent, small story I was 2 years old and I was amongst all my cousins and I guess somehow, I walked out the door to go and visit my Godmother across the alley. However, at the time she was in Pittsburg I found a group of older kids and decided I was going to play with them. My mother was scarred they all looked for me she says I was always so darn friendly with everybody I was well known so accurse she thought the worst. As she was ready to call the police My mom said she heard my voice My mom called out and I came running along with the other kids I found to play with. I got a spanking and finally my mom's tears stopped I guess we cried together. She tells me she knew then I was going to make it I was bold and nothing could stop me.

At the time my mom was a single mother living in Los Angeles, in an area called the Jungles, also known as the J's, and boy that was exactly what it was like survival daily. It was hard for kids in that area, we had crack heads, gang bangers, prostitutes, drive bye' and police. We lived in a very popular and raw area in the J's called Sherm Alley. This was in the 80's.

My mom lived at home with her family until I was 7 years old. We lived in a two-bedroom apartment, upstairs with most of my cousins also living there. It was hard I guess. I always stood out amongst the other kids. My mom sent me to a school called Sherman Oaks Elementary with a lot of wealthy kids, I was bused there, and I didn't belong their either. These kids had maids and butlers, lived in houses, and had both parents in the home, most of the kids that went there did. My mom was receiving welfare, need I say more. This farther made me more of an outsider. So, I created this story one time my aunt and uncle brought my mom to the school and I told my friends they were the driver and maid its funny now but then it wasn't.

I have a lot of memories some that made me laugh and some that made me sad. The weekends were the best part of my life. I visited my Grandparents on my Father's side. I was the Princess with them, the only girl, and my Grandmother loved me to death. My father had 3 brothers and 1 sister. His brothers were always in my life, my protectors. I thought they were the coolest people. My aunt was the most beautiful kindest woman I ever came across. My Father was on drugs and absent from my life so I didn't really know him. I remember seeing him two times, both times he showed up at my grandmother's house with a girlfriend in trouble. I was happy to see him each time, and also not so happy. He was always so aggressive, the "I'm your daddy" role but didn't know me. His siblings tried to make up for his absence by picking me up every weekend. The happiest memories of my childhood, going to church, and shopping with my Grandmother. My Grandparents were the only ones who I remember that went out of there way for Dirty Red (from both sides).

In 1987 my mother moved downstairs into her own apartment, that was major for my little sister and I. We finally had our own space, although every now and again someone needed a place to stay and my mom would always open the door. We lived right next door to my Great Uncle Pig, who gave me my first job. I would collect his mail all week and on Monday I would get a $1.00, I was rich. A couple of times my cousins would try to steal my job but never got it. I was also known as The Bag Lady, that's what my mother called me. I collected mail, papers, anything I could put in a bag. It's crazy I still live out of bags until this day. I believe I developed this need to have ownership. The bags were mine and everybody knew it.

Moving on 1990 My mom moved into a new place around the corner on Gibraltar, The G Block. I was 10 years old, the last year I was something like a kid. That summer my father started reaching out to my mother. He was in jail and my mom was still single. He started calling daily and my mom would stay up talking to him as long as she could. It was exciting I guess I was a kid getting to know my dad at that time I would have taken him any way he came and we did. I remember the night we stayed up because he was getting out of jail at 12 a.m. (Boy we had no clue that we just brought in Dr. Evil The grand reaper). My dad, my real dad was coming home. I didn't know at that time he was on drugs, we would find that out down the line but here we go. My mom seems to be happy, we had a boyfriend and it was my dad. One day we had a sleepover, my cousin, my sister and me made my parents breakfast from leftover dinner and asked my dad to marry us, we were big fans of the Cosby Show so anything was possible. He said yes, and Sept 15th, 1990 my parents got married. It was a big wedding, another happy day, they were in love and I had a dad something I always wanted of my own.

The Sun Rises at Midnight

Notes

Lisa Jackson

Notes

DARK FALLS

My life was getting ready to take a turn for the worst. My dad decided that I wouldn't be a kid anymore. My mother and her best friend left to go to the store, my uncle passed out on the couch, and me, and my little sister in the room with my dad putting puzzle pieces together. That's when I heard the words that haunt me every day "DO WE MATCH." I was 10 and my sister was 6 and to this day I wonder why I asked what that meant. He put my little sister out of the room and ended my childhood. I was molested for 3 years by my father, the man I loved.

Bittersweet he taught me how to match, I mastered that skill. At 13 years old I fought back making it the last time he would put his hands on me sexually. He stopped touching me but instead dressed me inappropriately and figured out another way of abuse. Setting me up with young guys in jail, having them call the house for me. I remember we went to the prison one day and he had me visit this guy when I was 15 years old. That was my life.

Life for us was horrible but I learned to deal with it as I grew up, becoming more defiant. My mother didn't like me much she said it often, "I love you but I don't like you." I heard that almost all my life from her. I started dating guys way too old for me, but I just wanted to get saved. I was a young sexually active girl looking for a way out.

December 26, 1995, my dad was arrested and went back to jail. At the time I was dating this guy I really liked. That same year I started having these bad nightmares of my dad doing things to me, I was reliving it. I got worse and worst to the point I felt like I wanted to die, so I tried taking my life. I took some pills but it didn't work. Thank God, I'm still here. I wish I can say things got better but it didn't right away. I confided in my mother and it hurt her. She didn't want to believe my dad was that way, so she didn't.

A few months later I found out I was pregnant. I was 16 years old just told my secret not too long ago and now this more shame. As time went my mom developed hatred towards me, it was hard. She was extremely depressed and therapy was not helping. I was asked to change my story and at this point, I would do anything to be back in my mom's good grace so I did. I was then told we would be taken away and my baby would be taken from me. Why wouldn't I believe that to be true? It was hard but it's funny the Doctor I was seeing didn't buy it and chose not to see me anymore. Leaving me lost, so I refused to see any more Doctors for my mental issues. Never receiving any treatment needed from being molested. I just went on with my life dealing with more and more abuse. Hell, I thought that was my name for a while (You deserve the worst).

Notes

Lisa Jackson

Notes

PAINFUL LOVE

My kid's father had his own mental illness issues I just didn't know it then. He started out kind and very supportive of me and then one day we are having an argument and boom I just got the taste slapped out of me. Our fights progressed, it got worse and worse. I was pregnant, broke, embarrassed, and alone. I couldn't tell anyone I was being hit so I kept it to myself. So much was happening then the worse came I left to go see my friends and when I came back to my baby father's home he wouldn't open the door, that was the first time I slept outside. I was 5 months pregnant no jacket and no food. It was cool that night. It's funny my dad had a few friends in the neighborhood they were crack heads, I was so happy to see them, they went and got me a new jacket, food, and a pair of shoes. The next morning, he opened the door, honestly, I don't know if he felt bad for leaving me outside.

Why didn't I go back to my family? A number of reasons ran through my head I was alone, who did I have, I'm getting my ass kicked by someone I love, this is all apart of my I deserve it attitude. I wasn't worthy of good but my child was. I prayed and that day I called my grandmother and she came and picked me up, she didn't say anything but she could tell something was wrong. My grandmother took me to buy clothes, got my hair done, and we had lunch, she loved me, I asked her to take me back home and she did. I can tell she was heartbroken My grandmother didn't know I was being abused I never shared that with anyone. I went back and he wanted to fight, accusing me of cheating, poured water on my new hair due and clothes. We fought and then he locked me in the house, no gas, lights, phone, and no food for 3 hours. I was 16 and you know the only thing I was thinking was if I can get a job and help things will get better. The next day he was nice asking me to forgive him, I did I loved him.

The Sun Rises at Midnight

Notes

Lisa Jackson

Notes

WHY ME

I went to see my mom at my aunt's house, at the time my mother refused to go back home, and our power was off. I had spoken with my dad, while he was in prison, and he told me how to cut the power back on. I accidentally let the wires touch and electrocuted myself. Me and the baby were ok, and the power was back on.

6 months pregnant and all I know is I want the best for my baby, so I moved back in with my mom. My dad was still in jail and I brought my baby daddy with me. My mom hated his guts at the beginning, eventually, they loved each other but that came far down the line. I took more abuse then the most humiliating thing happened while trying to be intimate with my kids' father. He started freaking out because worms started coming out of me. There are no words to describe the way I was feeling in that moment. I ran to my mom and we went to the doctor. I was so scared for my baby and myself. I didn't know what to do or why worms were coming out of me. I had got what they called pinworms. They were coming out of me through my stool and rear end, now talk about trauma during pregnancy. That was worse than getting hit. Now nobody

wants me to sit near them or be around them. It was so hard but I made it through.

December 25th at Christmas dinner I go into labor. The contractions got worse, the pain was real I couldn't take it anymore. We had no car, no one wanted to give us a ride so my mother and I caught the bus to the hospital. I finally made it to the hospital and a few hours later I had my beautiful baby girl. My kids' father didn't come, my mom didn't tell him until after I had the baby. It was a difficult time, more fights at home and now every time I try and go back to school it's a problem. I had no childcare so I never finished high school. I put it far behind me, the only thing I prayed for was to get a job, I couldn't wait until I turned 18.

Notes

Lisa Jackson

Notes

GET THE JOB

February 6, 1998, my birthday, I walked into this office to interview for a job. The position was to be a CEO of this company all I knew was in the paper it said no experience needed, and paid training. I made 18 years old that day, it was the first real job I ever tried to get and I didn't need permission from my mom. I was independent, that's what 18 meant to me, and finally, I can make decisions for me and my baby girl. I scheduled a few job interviews for that day, I figured no one was celebrating my birthday and I was right, no cake, another reason I wanted a job so that I may be able to do things. This job said to earn up to 6 figures. I was so excited so when I got there I looked around and it was a lot of young people there for the same position dressed in suits. I had on a white dress shirt and black pants and my hair in a bun. I started speaking to this one young lady who looked so nervous, I smiled and said "what are you worried about" she said "look around these are all college grads" I said to her "oh was that a requirement" she said "no it's just that I went to school with a few of these guys." I was not afraid I was thinking Oh well I don't know anyone here, they were all holding briefcases and folders I only had a pen and my purse. I walked up to the secretary and asked where the job application for me to feel out is and she smirked and said: "where is your resume." PAUSE Ok folks I was 18 years old and I didn't know what that was I thought it was saying something completely different when you see the movie you will laugh maybe not it's pretty sad well I sat back down and when I looked up everyone but me was called in. I was like ok, and then finally this guy comes out and calls me I was like wow why didn't the secretary call me like she called everyone else. (that wow was in a tone of fear). The gentleman says "Lisa Jackson come in please" I got up and walked up to him and held my hand out to shake his hand. I looked him in the eye and smiled saying "hello how are you" he smiled back and said "why thank you I am doing well and you," I said, "I'm here so I believe I'm doing well too." Then he said "have a seat" I'm like ok shaking inside but I did not want him to know. Then he looked me in the face and said "why are you here? Tell me a little about yourself." I said, "well today is my birthday, I'm 18 today" he was drinking water I think he almost spits it out. I can tell he was taken back. He said, "Happy Birthday are you serious?" I said, "yes sir It's my birthday." He said, "No that you're 18 today?" I said "yes." He then said, "do you even know what a CEO is?" I said, "honestly sir No but I am a quick learner I'm sure I will get the hang of it quickly plus your ad said paid training." He looked at me and was very quiet I said: "do you still want to hear about me?" He said, "I have a moment yes." I said, "I have always tried to get work but I was too young and needed my mom to fill out a permission sheet but because I had my daughter," he said, "stop right there you have a child?" I said, "yes she just made 1 in December." He dropped his head and said, "I have children your age." I said, "really sir well I am a mom and I need to take care of my baby, so I am here." He said, "Lisa, unfortunately, I can't give you the position as CEO but hold on you boldly walked in here with confidence." I said "well I prayed yesterday if I could get a job for my birthday I called your office after and they said to come in so I did my family don't think I will get the job but I said I'm going so I am here but I get it you don't want to give me the job I understand I'm too young." He said, "Hold on Ms. Jackson." I said "ok." He wrote a number down and said: "call this number." I did it turned out to be a security company, well I ended up not getting the CEO job but instead I was hired at the Security company. Yes, he made a call and they hired me they even took care of all my expenses, bus pass, uniform, shoes, and guard card. I was so excited I had to get on the bus and head straight over, I did and I got a job that day. It's funny I don't remember The CEO name but I remember how he said: "keep going don't give up."

Lisa Jackson

Notes

The Sun Rises at Midnight

Notes

PREGNANT AGAIN

I was showing up to work but then suddenly there were no shifts for me. My kid's aunt told me that her company was hiring so I went and I got the job, another security job. It was cool but I started feeling sick, tired, and I was constant pain. There were a lot of fights between me and my baby's father so he started not showing up to the house on time for me to go to work. Then I realized I missed my cycle so I went to the ER and found out I was pregnant again. I was torn because things were so bad at home and on top of that a few months ago I had an abortion, it was a 2-day procedure, the worst thing in the world. I was 17 and just going through so much at home. My kid's father didn't want another baby either and I was so sick at the time. My mom just kept saying "You don't need another baby you barely can take care of this one." Well, it's interesting, I went to the Doctor, they did an ultrasound and a few tests. They said something wasn't right, they saw abnormality with the baby. Well, I made the decision to end my pregnancy, it was horrible.

Fast forward, I'm pregnant again and torn so I prayed. My mother was pregnant at the time and went into labor on April 10th 1998. I hadn't told anyone other than my daughter's father and his sister, I wasn't sure what I was going to do so I kept quiet. When I showed up at the hospital my mom had just had my little brother. I held him and I knew I was having a baby again. I looked at my mom and said: "I'm pregnant." She looked at me like she was so out of it and she was, but I knew I was keeping my baby no matter what. I moved out of my mother's and into my first apartment across the street with my daughter's aunt as a roommate. It was another difficult pregnancy, he would always hit me or say, "That's not my kid!" Needless to say, he wasn't there for me but I always tried to see the good in him, so I tried to force him to be in our life. He still never went to any of the Dr. Appointments.

November 30th, 1998 a huge fight is happening "Stop putting your hands on me!" I said so many times, whispering because I didn't want anybody to know we were fighting. Even though I'm sure they knew. He was high and drunk as usual, "Get off me!" A lot of cursing and now I have just been pushed off the bed. I'm angry and crying, I get up and liquid is running down my leg. Now I'm feeling contractions, I say "Stop I think I'm wet!" He says "Your nasty ass pissed yourself again?" I said, "No asshole it's the baby!" I move again and more trickles came down, I knock on my parent's door but they didn't get up. He went and laid down, I'm in pain and pissed off, I walk outside and more fluid, my water broke finally. I get taken to the hospital, arriving at 3 a.m. on December 1st.

Finally, on December 1st at 4:17 pm my baby boy is here. it was the most difficult labor I had. On top of that, the Dr wanted to have my baby's father removed because he was being so mean to me. Plus no one from my family was there, it was sad. After that day he never came back to the hospital and I was fine with that.

My baby looked different, we both looked like he was beaten with bruises. Blood vessels had erupted in my eyes from fighting and having my baby. The hospital kept us for a few days and then we went home. My break is over back to hell. I now have a new baby, no job, and of course this guy not looking for work so it's on me.

Notes

Lisa Jackson

Notes

DO WHAT I HAVE TO DO

I get word from a good friend that her patient is looking for another caregiver, she lives in Santa Monica and the job pays weekly. My baby is a week old but we are broke and it's Christmas time. I got the job, but I was told not to expose that I had a newborn so I didn't. It was Winter, and I only had a sweater. I worked from 7 p.m. to 7 a.m. For the first week, I remember it was when they wanted to get rid of Clinton, I was only off on Sunday. I received 1 check and felt like it was worth it during that week.

My chest started hurting and swelling up. The milk was not coming out I tried everything to get it out but couldn't. I developed a horrible cough that I couldn't get rid of for 2 weeks. On Sundays I showed up to the ER, the first time I received a shot and a Lactaid nurse spoke to me about breastfeeding. I explained I don't breastfeed she told me I should. I needed to pump and get that milk out. I went home in pain barely could lift my arms and on top of that, there was a huge lump growing in my breast. My baby is now 3 weeks old and I can't hold him. The next night I get a call "Lisa don't come in." I'm like good "But Why?" My patient said "You are such a sweet young lady and Thank you for trying to care for me but I have lived a long great life you need to take care of yourself. You are ill, don't come back you are fired." Thank you, Ms. Rose, you were right the next day I wake up unable to move, the pain is horrible, my neck is pulsating, my chest has turned blue black purple and green, and was so huge. The ambulance is called, I'm taken to the ER and It is not considered an emergency to them, I'm just another patient wasting their time with Medi-cal. That's actually what a nurse said that's what I get said that nurse, "These fast ass girls out here having kids and can't take care of them." I guess she didn't care I could hear what she was saying. Now I'm in the fast track where they take vitals and the nicest nurse comes in, I'm crying tears falling from embarrassment and pain. She says "Baby what's going on?" I tell her "I been here for hours and this is my 3rd visit and nobody has helped me and now they want to send me home again to go to urgent care instead." She says "Sit here hun." (I'm like Look where am I going) She then says "Where are your parents?" I said, "I don't know I came here in the ambulance." Then she says "Just follow my lead." I said "Ok." She calls the Dr and says, "This patient is refusing to leave until she is seen by you, she doesn't want anyone else but the head doctor on the floor." It's funny because He was actually headed to lunch to meet his wife, I remember him talking in the hallway where they had me sitting for 3 hours. He came and I was getting worst I started sweating bad and shaking. He walks in and says "What's wrong?" I open my shirt and his face dropped. He walked away without touching me and yells "Nurses get over here look at this!" I'm like what then at that very moment I hear cursing, my dad is out there asking where I am, I hear him I tell the nurse that was so kind "That's my father out there." She said "Oh Lord."

My dad came in and he sees me with my shirt open and a growth out my chest that looks like it's about to burst. All of a sudden, I am getting prep for emergency surgery, yes, I was dying it was so much infection. Here is the next blessing, a plastic surgeon happens to be there and he was doing some charity work. Where he does special cases for people who can't afford insurance and he heard about me while he was there and he asked if he could perform my surgery. I didn't care who did it as long as I was out of pain. Imagine your breast dark and so big, the nipple has gone, it's completely discolored and 5 sizes larger from swelling. The pain was so real that the wind even hurt. I asked him one thing, as they all kept apologizing to me, "will I have my breast after this?" He smiled and said, "I will take care of you don't worry." Sure enough, he did Thank You DR. I wake up in recovery and that was so painful, my breast could not be closed, I had an abscess the size of a softball in my chest. My breast milk had produced but could not flow out my duct glands because they are underdeveloped; the milk was spoiling on the inside of me. I was saved but now, I can't hold my son for about a month because I needed to heal. God had me that's all I can say. Eventually, I got better and went on with life.

Lisa Jackson

Notes

Notes

DISLOCATED NOSE

That summer my kids' father and I had the biggest fight, he punched me in my face, hitting my nose, and blackening my eye with one hit. Blood was everywhere. He hit me in front of my babies. I was made fun of by my family and friends and I knew we were coming to an end. I woke up one night out my sleep and had to choose him or me, I chose me. I got a job with plans to move on. One month in the plan I collapse on my floor while getting ready for work. I wake up in the hospital with an IV in my arm and tubes with my pastor standing over me praying, Bishop Miquel. As I write I remember each time I was in the hospital he was standing over me praying. It turns out I had an infection in my pancreas, and gallbladder from gallstones. They had to perform emergency surgery on me again to remove the stones and based on when they go in they will see just how bad it was. God had me again because the stones had traveled all around my pancreas. I survived yet another thing. I was released from the hospital 3 weeks later, I returned home on the 1st, my baby boy's birthday, it had been awhile since I saw my babies I missed them. It was also my new beginning because my relationship was truly over. He never came to the hospital to check on me and when I got home he walked in and placed my baby right on my womb, I cried but it was over December 1st, 1999.

Lisa Jackson

Notes

Notes

ANGRY SINGLE MOM

Thank you, Jesus. I wish I could have said that then. I had so much to learn about how good God was and is. I was able to return to my job after I healed and I moved back in with my parents on a mission to get my own. I really did not want to be there but that is where I was. I had two kids and I was only 19 years old, that was a sad Christmas for me, but I thank God, I was still here to make sure the next Christmas would be good.

Time went on I reached out for help with the kids and he never would respond. I learned my kids only had me, so when I worked my friends and parents would keep my kids then finally one day he called me and wanted to talk. I was up to it so we met in the alley and he was extra nice that day. I thought odd but ok he asked: "We cool?" I said "Yes." it was two days before I got paid and I asked him what he was doing later he said "Nothing." I said I was planning on ordering some food for me and the kids, and told him the baby needed diapers, he had four left. He said out the blue "I will get them." I'm like what really ok I said: "Are you sure?" He said, "Yes go and order pizza." I said, "I don't have enough for pizza."

He said, "I got it." I'm like ok we ordered the food then he said I will be right back. I didn't think anything of it, long story short he left, I mean literally left, he moved to Vegas and said nothing. The delivery people showed up and my friend Gabby paid what I was short. I called his friend's house and that's how I found out he just pulled off with his friends headed to Vegas. I asked, "Did he at least get the diapers?" No, he just left, I screamed I was angry, hurt, and ashamed. I couldn't deal anymore, that was it for me, something happened and I don't know if it was a good thing or bad. An angry young mother that had prayed for help but instead things got worse. Everything was falling apart on top of that the company I worked for moved and didn't tell anyone, I was mailed my last check. It's crazy now I'm back with no job again, and I'm pissed. I keep getting into fights at home with my parents, and now my dad has struck a nerve. I remember that day, he was being himself, rude and abusive to my mom, I told him "Do you ever stop damn?" He said, "Bitch who the fuck you talking to?" I said "You Bitch!" He said, "You can get out!" I said, "I'm not going anywhere!" He said, "Yes you are!" Then he grabs my baby and sets her on the other side of the front door. I go into a rage and go for his computers. I tried to destroy his things. He rushes me pushing me into the table I fall over everything and it's like the royal rumble. I moved out that day and moved in with my grandparents', which was the year 2000, now I have no job and two kids.

Lisa Jackson

Notes

The Sun Rises at Midnight

Notes

THE COUNTY BUILDING

Now I'm on my way to the county building in need of help and I need it quick! This place is the worse place to go if you are looking for a picker upper. The kids and I are here, I'm trying to fill out all these papers on my own, it's so much, on top of that we were there the entire day with no money. We're so miserable, it's so many people here, the lines are so long, its worst then the DMV and its so much negative attitude. Why is everyone angry and rude? I'm talking about the social workers again. I'm scared to walk out, they may call my name. Why do these workers feel they need to be so aggressive, and nasty to us, the people here need help that's why most us are here? I mean I take no pleasure in being here at all, free money my ass this is worse than prostitution. Pimps treat hoes better than the treatment you get from this place.

They call me "Lisa Jackson." "I'm here." "Ok, Ms. Jackson sign here. Here is $200.00 of emergency funds you will hear from us in 30 days ok." Never been so happy to leave a place, I was ready to lose it. I look at my kids and say "I'm sorry>" I cried, I was a failure, I was in this place again needing assistance, with $200.00

to last for 30days and 2 kids. Lord, please help me! My time went on and I was determined to do better. I was told about a program called Crystal Stairs and they could help me with childcare so I went there. I filled out paperwork and I qualified for the program, a load lifted off my shoulders. Now I just need a job and someone I trust to help keep my kids. Well I was so happy I was on my way, kids can go to daycare. I was so excited, help finally, now get a job. I looked and looked but nothing came through, eventually, I was approved for TANF and then I received a letter scheduling me for the welfare to work program. I was ready for a change I needed it but I really didn't want to be beaten down more however I went. I'm 20 years old with 2 kids not married Lord do you hear me.

I didn't know then he did hear me he was always setting me up for blessings.

Lisa Jackson

Notes

Notes

NOT GIVING UP

I'm in the gain welfare to work program sitting there saying to myself "I don't want to be here these people treat you as if you are beneath them like we are nothing." Well if I'm here I will get all I can out of this. My babies were waiting for me to fix our lives and I'm clueless about what steps to take. I'm just moving from place to place mentally with 1,000 thoughts going on at once. The main one is "Lisa you're the smart one that always falls short something must give what you going to do." And then the worker walks in "Today class we are working on goals, so let's start with do you know how to fill out a job application?" You should see the reaction of the people faces in this class. I remember one guy said "This is a joke!" and walked out angry. I know I was feeling like the world was on my shoulders, I got babies period so I have to sit here. I looked for the positive like maybe they will give us the right things to say or what not to say and sure enough they did, they had like a cheat sheet for example instead of saying you became pregnant is the reason you left your previous job say family planning. I met a lot of awesome people during the program, it lasted for two weeks and during that time we were to look for work daily. I was excited about that part, find work was my focus, school at the time was out the picture, I needed money to take care of my kids and $550.00 a month with two kids wasn't doing it. I know I can do better, I told myself that and I knew it. The most interesting thing is I know a lot of women that would rather stay in the sorry system then take a chance and get out here and clock in. Here is the truth it's like crack you can become dependent on that little bit and know that each month as long as you do your part you have the amount you know you're supposed to get, compared to getting a job, losing the job, and nothing coming in. The system is what I was raised on, I remember I use to dream of having section 8, lol, cheap rent and life support. I never in my life had section 8 and you know what I am so thankful I was unable to get it. I instead worked hard for everything I got.

Anyway, two weeks went by and the class was over I left with three things bus tokens, a certificate of completion, and a reminder that if anyone hired a person that received Tanf food stamps then that could be tax-exempt $10,000, a little incentive to hire people like us.

It was fall of 2000 and at this point, I wasn't giving up. I had tokens and found out that s department store was hiring for seasonal workers. I went and filled out my app and was dressed for an interview. God's grace that day the manager was there and was the person passing out applications. I had spoken to her and she interviewed me right then, told me I had to pass the background and drug test, which I did and received the job, Thank you, Jesus. I called my grandmother to give her the great news. I started and it wasn't long before they asked me did I want to stay on as a permanent employee. I took the job after Christmas hours dropped I couldn't keep up with all my responsibilities; it was part-time work, not enough money. So, I started looking for new employment, one day I was at a local mall and found out they were hiring so I went and applied for a job and was hired right away, a blessing. I, unfortunately, gave my two-week notice to the department store, glad I did they closed the business shortly after that, leaving a lot of people out of work. Thank you, Jesus, for sending me elsewhere. Now I'm working my new job meeting a lot of new awesome people and enjoying what I do. Of course, it started getting difficult with rides, I got off late and it started to become extremely difficult with getting home, no car, and I didn't know how to drive but I kept going.

 Moving on as far as performance I was doing well at my job, I just made 21, and I met one of my close friends there, Fabby my beautiful friend, she trained me and left, yes, she quit. It was like she was there just for me God placed her in my life we became so close sisters for life. Funny how God brings people together. My dear sweet beautiful friend Fabby. you are an amazing woman don't ever let anything stop you from being just that amazing Love you.

Notes

Lisa Jackson

Notes

MARRIAGE

I stayed with that company and ended up getting promoted to my own department. I'm full time now, things are turning around financially. I still wanted a complete family. I was on lunch one day and saw this guy in line in the food court. I wanted to say Hi so I left the line I was in and went to the line he was in and sure enough, he saw me and he allowed me to get in front of him. He then said, "Hi where is your husband." I was like "No husband very single." We exchanged numbers, he called and we started talking, and dating, it was moving so fast. He was nice to me, which was better than the treatment I was getting. He was everywhere I needed him to be, he would show up at my job before I got off just to make sure I was safe. He met my kids and my family right away we were good, I thought.

    I finally moved into my first apartment by myself and I looked up and he was at the door with his things, moving in. I was on top of the world someone who wanted to help me. I dismissed the jealousy, the fact that he was always uncomfortable with anyone who said anything to me. I just wanted to be somebody's, so I ignored the signs as time went on he got more aggressive, we argued more and more, then my family had a party and we went. He acted crazy and took me home and went back to the party leaving me home. When he came in drunk and angry and wanted to get fresh we had not been intimate in months we argued and he placed his hand around my throat and squeezed I tried fighting back except my eyes got blurry and I passed out the next morning I was naked on the floor I asked him to leave he did 2 months later I was sick in the ER and found out 2 hours before my birthday I was pregnant Yes I'm at MLK ER and I'm in a wheelchair on my way to get x-rayed and someone is running down the aisles screaming no x-ray stop We stopped and was like what's going on, bring her back well when I was brought back to the room I was told there to take another pee test and so I did but it was so painful on my side and they sat me in the room and said congratulations you're pregnant I was speechless and let me tell you it was the longest ride with my grandmother ever. I was told I was having another baby 2 hours before I made 22 years old 3 kids well at least this time I had my own place the only problem was I wasn't working anymore I stayed with that employer a short while my son became very ill and I had to care for him I missed too many days and fell right back into the trap of woe is me, boy satan is always working to destroy, so much I didn't know then I write this to be of help to many I have had my share of heartbreaking moments that is why I wear my smile so big today people always ask me why I smile so much and I say to myself they don't know the tears behind this smile it's God's unfailing love. I'm 22 and this pregnancy is hard I barely can walk but I did my boyfriend checked out often we were on and off the entire pregnancy I was so use to mistreatment it was so common for me nothing went well so I decided I had to have been cursed I must come from a line of second best you know used and only new to the purchaser that was my sad beliefs but you know I never wanted people to know that's how I felt about myself. I was a lemon well I did have a beautiful baby boy and ended up marrying his father 2 months later in a chapel on Vermont no one from his family showed up and a handful of mine was there It was a moment in my life I won't forget I know now that when something is blessed by God it won't be forced it will come so naturally and in order, because He is a God of completion and order. Nothing against my ex-husband I pray many blessings over his life we just weren't ready however I learned from that relationship so much our marriage had so many obstacles cheating was the least of our problems see the end of our marriage my ex didn't want my son around our son see in 2003 my 4 year old dropped my 10 month old out of the window of the second floor our baby survived but our marriage didn't I'm totally ok with our ending we tried to stay together but we stayed constantly at each other's throat we both stepped out in the relationship Him way before me but 2 wrongs don't make it right at all. We were young and selfish we both wanted the same thing we just did not know how to articulate our needs towards each other it just continued to go downhill he became way more abusive crazy drinking and smoking drugs played a big part him doing them was the problem that was a deal breaker for me to the cheating that was my way out you ever love someone but at the same time want them far away from you I tell you this we did 1 thing right that beautiful little boy we gave life to I love him so much no regrets at all with all that I know I would do it all again for him. Mommy loves you.

I stayed married for 10 years before the divorce was final it was ugly but everything happens for a reason God was always in control leading me to better even though I constantly tried to do it myself.

Lisa Jackson

Notes

Notes

HOPE

2003 February 6 it was my 23rd birthday and I walked in a dental office for an interview that my cousin told me about, at that time it was very difficult for us I had just recently had my 3rd child just married and broke my husband was working but it was hard to find consistent work he was an illegal immigrant so it was always under pay, and odd jobs but God always made a way. I was recovering from a very difficult pregnancy which was something that came common for me, however, I was doing better I prayed Lord I need a job and that weekend, I saw my cousin which I didn't see often but my best friend and her were living in the same home at the time and in conversation my cousin expressed how they were looking for a front office person to schedule appointments and answer phones I said to myself I could do that I asked her a little more about the job and here is the funny thing she says hey Lisa your sister left the job you should come apply but don't tell them you know me I'm like my sister she says yes she quit lol I'm like well that's her choice when should I show up she said Friday is the open appointments call Thursday and say you saw the Add in the LA Times.

I called I was scheduled and I showed up with one thing on my mind get the job rent is coming up so I caught the bus to 4th and Fairfax near the Grove I was a little intimidated by the atmosphere everyone looked expensive like they just jumped out a magazine I had on my church clothes that didn't fit well I just had a baby but I tried. As I walked in and a lady was walking out she looked amazing like she knew she had the job I was like all damn well Lisa you came this far don't turn back now I took a deep breath and I prayed God please don't be mad I'm going to act like I don't know my fam just help me get the job so I kept saying to myself if I don't get the job we will be homeless NO this can't happen to us I got this. I looked up and Chris my fam is standing there with a straight face she says Hi how can I help you I almost forgot that quick and said hey Chris lol she looked at me like girl I was like oop oh-oh I wiped the smile off my face and said Hello I am here to interview for the front office position with a smile on her face she says hold on one moment let me get the doctor. Dr. Z came out tall beautiful blonde hair white girl with the biggest smile and says where is your resume I gave it to her and she started asking me questions mainly why I came to her office I expressed I was looking for work and didn't want to pass on this opportunity I had experience in customer service I was great at that we connected Dr. Z and I and then she said these words why should I hire you out of all the qualified applicants and you have a cavity in between your 2 front teeth with no dental experience at all. I was on a mission get a job and take care of your family that was my mission I said I am a quick learner and I will get my teeth fixed however if you let me walk out of here it will be your biggest mistake ever... I said that out loud oh my God what did I just do that's what I was thinking after I looked Dr. Z in the face well I got the Job.

All I know is the good Lord put favor on me no other reason there were other qualified people as far as background and experience in dentistry and she choose me the black girl with a cavity.

Dr. Z at the time was the most amazing woman I had met in my life She was a Dr. with her own business and she blessed me with a job I had no idea at the time that God would use this woman to help guide me in the direction of my dreams. Dr. Z had love for her team as we had love for her we were a family one I was proud to be a part of, so 1 day she came in the office and said we would be closed for 3 days we were going to a fortune management class I was like what I had no clue what she was talking about so I asked the mom of the business Mrs. E she says quietly you will like it with sarcasm I was excited that's all I know I was so happy at that time all I could dream of was help Dr. Z be the best Dentist in the world I was 23 from the hood so it was easy for me to hustle so I did and then it happened we arrived at a hotel and there were lots of other dental practices there they asked us to be seated and this guy comes out with energy I never seen before He was this big tall white dude with 1 focus and you could tell his focus was to get us to believe his way worked He was wealthy needless to say and he was what you call a life coach he had a sports car he talked about his accomplishments and blahblahblah and how this guy named Tony Robbins changed his life and then he played a video Stop first off I was the only person in the room that did not know who the hell Tony Robbins was all I knew was when I first heard him speak I was alert and receptive to the information a lot said was common sense just put in a different way however I listened I didn't miss a beat I had to use the restroom and I held it because I didn't want to miss anything I mean the room was on fire, between our assigned life coach to Tony Robbins next to church I never been in a room so turned up with a focus to have a better life. Moving on I knew right then I wanted to speak I was thinking oh my God people pay to hear somebody talk it's like a concert just speaking instead lol. It was there that I thought just maybe I was in the right place at the right time the only problem was instead of believing in myself to accomplish goals I was believing in Dr. Z and that through her my blessings would come so I started dreaming of how if I could help her accomplish her dream my life could get better see I still had the mentality that great things and riches only happen to others just not me that I could always just be the help assistant not the head honcho and that thinking stayed with me for a while. I didn't know what I know now, working in that office I was exposed to different things that most people where I came from didn't even talk about hell nobody in my family ever spoke about toastmasters honestly, I thought it was about wine and giving toast. when I was first asked would I like to attend a meeting a patient of ours asked me He brought me in Dr. Z thought it would be great if I could speak better to our patients and I wanted to be better I wanted more for my family at the time me doing better would also be a part of the destruction of my marriage the better I did the more my husband cheated and hated my guts it's funny he was jealous, the thought that I might realize I could actually do better silly of him I thought we were doing better. moving on, its 2005 a lot of things are going wrong, patients and money wasn't happening the way Dr. Z wanted the place was divided personal issues were entering the workplace the enemy came in to destroy none of us was ready for what was to come, a meeting took place and things were said, long story short that day was the last day I would be working for Dr. Z It was the saddest day of my life I no longer looked at my employer as that, instead I looked at her as my friend betraying, and blaming me, saying things I didn't like at that time I lost my cool I spoke in such a way I was not proud I was extremely disrespectful I spoke the same way my dad spoke to us when he was angry I learned the hard way that no matter what I feel I should never hit a low point and behave the way I did because of hurt feelings I was 25 and I acted like a child I could say it was justified but it was not I didn't know better I just knew how to fight back when pushed up against a wall. That day I acted a fool but worst I lost my friend someone I looked up to, I hurt her with the sword my tongue. Although many years has gone by, I still miss her from time to time and Mrs. E moments when I wish I could give her a call just to say Hi being right should never mean you lose your relationships I would learn that down the line. Dr. Z just know I love you and I am truly sorry for the pain I caused you during that time.

Notes

Lisa Jackson

Notes

A LEAP OF FAITH

A powerful moment for the kids and I 2005 something great happened to the kids and me it was 7 a.m. and I was cleaning house I said to my daughter today we getting a car she looked at me like I was crazy, I was. We had our cleaning clothes on comic was all over me with a headscarf on I remember something came over me all I knew was the car I had was not safe for my kids so I moved I took them to breakfast because the dealership was not open yet then we sat outside waiting long story short we left our other car parked on the street and we went home with our new Jeep I felt on top of the world that day my daughter was so excited she looked at me like mom look what you did I was Thanking Jesus the entire time. Even in the middle of my storms God always gave me moments of sunlight.

Lisa Jackson

Notes

Notes

MY SELF-WORTH

I entered more troubling relationships 1 after another. I even convinced myself they loved me when all awhile they only loved what I can do for them. I didn't know my self-worth I walked around as if I deserved pain as if I deserved to be second best or last pick. I was in some pretty bad relationships 5 to be exact I called it my fav 5. The Liar, The Entertainer, The Boss, The Biker and the 5th was anybody to fill the void of my emptiness. The Liar was the DJ/Truckdriver who for the life of me just could not be truthful but he made me laugh, I mean laugh we had fun together he was so charming even though his ass was always lying. He was seeing me, and his sister's best friend. It's funny how I found out I saw his sister who I was cool with no drama his entire family was wonderful full of laughs anyway I saw her in the club while I was with my friends and just in casual conversation she let me know she didn't want to be in the middle anymore. I was clueless to what she was talking about and she said I love you both but he will not make a decision, so I am telling you my brother is seeing my best friend, and you Lisa. You both are amazing women I love, and I don't want to hurt you but the truth is the truth. I was sitting there feeling humiliated, yet honestly, I knew it was someone else. If I was so wonderful why couldn't we move forward. Well as you know he lied, and denied, he even blamed me accused me of the worst things because I was at the club. That relationship went on and off for years. But that night was pretty much the end we were never to laugh the same. Moving forward let's talk about The Entertainer the man that made me feel like I was a woman, like I could do anything. This man brought out something in me I really didn't like but it didn't matter I just wanted to give this man the key to my world, I didn't want to disappoint him. Honestly, I am still trying to figure out why but let's just say He had the magic touch and all the ladies stood in line for it. I mean I was one of many there for him, in a competition that I was better than the next. A scary trap. Thursday through Sunday Repping my man and proud. I wanted to be the perfect woman so no complaining, no getting upset. He didn't realize just how much I was for him His lies were so unnecessary. I didn't care about the fans it was a part of his life our life the life we would have together. That's what I told myself hahaha the joke was on me, years of hurt I was always for him but he was never for me. Then we had The Boss the street entrepreneur 16-year difference in age hell his daughter and I was born the same year. My Frank Locus I wanted to be the main his bottom as they call it he was here today and gone tomorrow always on the grind his life was not good for my kids it was dangerous so I kept them separate. It never crossed my mind that I should have never been in his world at all but I so wanted acceptance. Baby no calls I'm working you know I don't take that cell with me it will get me caught up the rules no contact I will contact you. What a life but with him I would have no financial worries. And now The Biker or should I say the time traveler This dude boy I was trapped with this one never keeps his word disappear at any time with the most bogus excuses baby give it time baby I'm sorry baby I have to work full of shit ass man he was also 16 years older than me. As you can see I was hurting, and struggling with my self-worth the truth is the spirits was on me. I was drawing wicked because I felt dirty from my youth I was troubled. I stayed in these horrible relationships because I thought this was my worth a single woman with children I was unwanted not worthy of being chosen so I did what I thought was needed to keep the wrong folks in my life. I got tired I was a praying woman so i asked The Lord to help me change to bless me, to give me my Boaz, and then I said no it won't ever happen for me. So, I kept right on attracting the worst I wasn't really ready for what I was praying for I didn't realize how faith really worked. My faith had conditions the conditions was it could happen for others just not me. Thank you, Lord Jesus, for not holding me to my thoughts.

Notes

Lisa Jackson

Notes

THE STROKE

Satan came for me but in a different way, I remember I would always meet people in passing and they would say do you know the story of Job. I heard about him but never actually read the story myself. That would come down the line. I know now God wanted to get my attention and boy did he. He put me in time out I was killing myself, that self-destruct mode I talked about earlier. I was in autopilot work was stressful but good, I was making more money, I had my home, my kids, and my car I was good so I thought. I never realized just how God always kept us, my relationships were horrible, but I was in thoughts that I needed help looking back I always took care of my kids without the help of the men I was the one always working and providing for my kids, not the men. I was blinded, but anyway I was at work one day and my arm felt funny like dead weight a tingling feeling I had my charts in my hand one second then the next everything was on the floor my arm was numb My co-worker happens to be walking pass on break and she was on the phone with her dad who worked at the hospital she said hey are you ok I said not sure I feel weird my arm is numb her dad asked her what was going on she told him what I said he said I needed to go to the ER so I did, I drove myself to the ER and all I remember is while talking my speech started to slur and I woke up in the hospital bed that was the most difficult time of my life. I was diagnosed with a mild stroke the stress of my demons had caught up with me I felt like the world was against me I was alone I couldn't do anything about it I got worse instead of better my entire right side had stop functioning I couldn't hold anything stand or see out my right eye it was a blur my face was dropped my speech slurred I could gather my thoughts at all nothing was right and I was 27 years old. I thought I was going to die so I threw in the towel I could not clean myself it was horrible and the doctors was clueless it was a lot of back and forth with my diagnosis then finally one doctor said minor stroke and that was that a lot of testing and therapy I didn't care what they called it I just wanted to die at this point. Then I get a visit from my good friend Nikki my other sister from God, and she walks in the hospital like I was ok she was sad but she kept it together and she said girl I can't wait until you get your ass up we got shit to do. She wiped my mouth off then she said how we go be in the club with you like this you know they be waiting for us to make our entrance we Hollywood. You know I never told her but that triggered something in me. I started telling myself this is not it for me I was released with a lot of follow-ups I lost everything my home and my kids was with family but the scar that remains my baby boy I could not care for him he was little so his dad went to divorce court for custody of the baby and boy was I then motivated my thoughts was I have to get better so I prayed for God to heal me I went to therapy physical and mental I started doing better each day was a struggle but I kept getting better I did everything they told me not to do or that I couldn't do then one day my face had turned back I was so happy the only problem was whenever I felt overwhelmed my face would turn crooked My doctor said I had a severe case of bell's palsy I tell this story to tell you never give up put your trust in God instead of things that have no power like I did I gave power to meaningless things. Things I had no control over I went through so many medical moments during that time. My body would just start jerking really hard I couldn't stop it, slur speech, and falling over when walking. My Girl was there for me Niki I Thank you for everything in my darkest hours you were there May God continue to shine on you my dear friend Slay as you always do. But to God be the glory I stand straight my speech is fine and I look great but it's still one day at a time. I look good on the outside, but I know The Good Lord is still fixing me on the inside.

Lisa Jackson

Notes

Notes

HEARTBROKEN

2009 I lose the man of my life, my Papa (Grandfather) He died of cancer I died too. I didn't care anymore He loved me and wanted the best for me that was a hard time for the family a lot of fighting happening but I was getting better I remember it was Valentine's day 2009 I prayed that night God help me I still had issues from the stroke my kids felt like I had abandoned them and my family helped them to believe that. I checked out period I never wanted my kids to see me doing so bad I was homeless it was crazy I just hated the fact that I had to rely on others period but that moment when I saw my Papa in such bad shape I got off the self-pity woe is me train, I said Jesus fix me I can't do it myself that very moment my Papa said come back home I didn't know then, but it was God. as I got better he got worse My grandmother cared for him alongside of her was me that was the last year of woe was me, but I first had to hit a couple more blocks. My great aunt came over to check on my grandmother and she had a book with her that book would change my life it was a daily devotional walking in Christ and then my cousin also came with a book 2 different times same week and they gave me the biggest blessings of my life I had not completely turned yet, my grandfather passed away May 2009 and I met the devil I started dating this man that would get me in the world of trouble I checked out and did something I can never take back I entered the adult entertainment business it was a short time. But My God is so good to this day he washed me clean of it I walk with my head high no weapon formed against me shall prosper even in that dark time I was covered with the blood I remember on 1 audition I was telling the girls about how good Jesus was they were looking at me like I was crazy and one said then why are you here. Thank God that was the last audition for me in that field, and the end of that relationship. A few months later I met a producer while shopping and He asked me to come out to a dance video audition a different direction I was like ok I got the info and I showed up. I was invited to the music video little to know that when I saw the crews and all that was involved something happened I wanted to make films I told myself I can do this, I can be a producer put things together to tell a story. I went there for 1 reason but God had a better plan for me.

Lisa Jackson

Notes

Notes

TALK ABOUT BEING SIFTED

2010 The producer and I became great friends I called him one day with an idea he said don't tell me go get your idea registered I didn't know what he was talking about he said the writers guild I was clueless but I didn't tell him I googled and saw the writers guild west and Yes I went and registered my idea and I mailed it to myself a few months later I called him back and said I did what you told me now are you ready to hear my idea I wanted to do reality TV he laughed with joy he said you are serious I'm like yes but I tried to schedule a meeting and the worse happened my son became very ill he was diagnosed with spinal meningitis I was so scared I had just asked to be a better mother. And a week later this, we spent a month in the hospital fighting for my sons life and I prayed God heal my child I stayed at that hospital and I didn't see my other kids they could not come see their brother it was so hard but we made it He got out the hospital 2 days before Easter and check this out God answered my prayers and my son was healed the doctors came in to say he was misdiagnosed they are unclear as to what caused all the symptoms but the last test ruled out meningitis again I don't care what they were talking God heard my cries my son was healed. We went to church it was Easter Sunday I was happy the church had been praying for my son also It was a happy moment for me then I looked up and the Biker was there my son was in the hospital for a month and he suddenly shows up now. I was different he just didn't know it I said Jesus help me change I deserve better You said.

Lisa Jackson

Notes

MY BOAZ

I completely forget about my request I go to church the following week with the decision this would be my last visit here. I was running late but it turned out I was on time. I walked in and there was standing a beautiful man he grabbed my hand to shake and he held on a lil bit we had a moment I went to my seat thinking who is that I need to know I had no idea that he was my Boaz I was just use to the wrong kind of guys I didn't really think I would get a good one I was no good But God knows the real me and saw different His name was Jim and we went on to date and he proposed to me in front of the congregation My dreams started to come to pass Spring 2010 we met and winter 2010 my Boaz proposed.

Lisa Jackson

Notes

THINGS BEGIN TO TURN AROUND

The beginning of a new chapter where great things happens for Lisa the change was my attitude the way I viewed myself. I continued on working on my reality show and other ideas I was confident I was being made over God had a vision for my life all I needed to do was agree and believe. 2010 Jim and I gave our lives over to Christ and something happened the favor I had all along I could now recognize. Jim and I started going to the Christian 12 step program at the Inglewood Salvation Army called Recovery Friday. Thank God for the amazing people he covered Jim and I with. The Lord surrounded us with love Mr. Gary, Mrs. Lisa, and Joe and Diane, Greg, The Montgomery's and many other's the love they showed us It was nothing but God. Stay connected they said, trust in the Lord they said lean not unto your own understanding they said. I had more confidence and it was real I placed my trust in God instead of the meaningless things. I was constantly being blessed growing in my faith.

Lisa Jackson

Notes

I'M WORTHY TO BE LOVED

Jim and I was married talk about love He stuck through tough times with me see what you don't know was I was physically being attacked I was ill my legs would give out often and I would just fall over or at sometimes he would have to carry me to our bed because my legs couldn't move my body would just shake my hands give out I would forget things and he never complained instead he just loved me Jim wanted kids and we tried but no success at the beginning. It took 4 years but God said yes and we had a son.

Lisa Jackson

Notes

I SEE LIGHT

Jim and I moved our family to Victorville a place everyone said don't go, well God said yes and let me tell you doors opened left and right I started a new job at the local superstore and 6-7 months later I was promoted to being a manager I started a group called the Barrier Breaking women with 1 thought. I wanted to positively impact other women I held a meeting where I invited my co-workers out and I stood in front of these ladies sharing a little of my story and how with just a change of attitude they could reach their dreams. Then bam God goes and blows my mind he blessed me with an opportunity that would change my life forever. A co-worker told Rosena about me Ms. Shay I thank you for letting God use you and being in the right place at the right time. Seasons of Change Bent Not Broken I met a woman who selflessly blessed me her name Rosena Flynn a woman whose heart is after God, Rosena invited me to speak amongst great speakers, she believed in me I still am in awe. I am just so thankful.

Lisa Jackson

Notes

Notes

GOD IS GOOD

I am at Season of change bent but not broken OMG we here its so many amazing people in the room telling their stories I am in aww taking notes not wanting to miss a beat and also scarred out my boots can they tell?

I was so nervous I'm thinking why would these people want to hear my story I am not rich what can I teach them and as I was ready to listen to Satan and his lies about me, there standing in the back of the room Dave Daily I don't know why I said anything to him, I was shaken on the inside I think he picked up on that, and he said it's your story You know it and it's your responsibility to tell it. Thank you well I spoke tears and a quiet room I received a standing ovation they received me. I have a new family sent from God I am now pursuing my dreams and Greg Walker the Big Dreamer said to me after hearing my story go write a #1 bestseller I said how? He said pick up a pen and write. Here it is Thank you. And this is how I know The Sun Rises at Midnight.

Notes

Lisa Jackson

Notes

AT MIDNIGHT

The Lord loves you and although you may feel alone and pained, the odds may be against you, just know that God is your vindicator He loves you and never intended for you to have to go through such a thing, you are precious. So, no matter what you are going through, you can know that the Lord is with you. He will bring you through

Psalm 138: 3

"In the day when I cried out, You answered me, and made me bold with strength in my soul."

Lisa Jackson

Notes

YOU ARE LOVED

Perfectly made in His image you should never be ashamed to be different. God made you perfect don't allow people to determine you.

Psalm 139: 13-16

For you formed my inward parts; you knitted me together in my mother's womb. I praise you, for I am fearfully and wonderfully made. Wonderful are your works; my soul knows it very well. My frame was not hidden from you when I was being made in secret, intricately woven in the depths of the earth. Your eyes saw my unformed substance; in your book were formed for me, when as yet there was none of them.

Lisa Jackson

Notes

KEEP GOING

1Chronicles 28:20

Then David said to Solomon his son, "Be strong and courageous and do it. Do not be afraid and do not be dismayed, for the Lord God, even my God, is with you. He will not leave you or forsake you, until all the work for the service of the house of the Lord is finished.

Proverbs 3: 5-6

Trust in the Lord with all your heart, and do not lean on your own understanding. In all your ways acknowledge him, and he will make straight your paths

Lisa Jackson

Notes

CONTACT INFORMATION

For Speaking or Support You can contact me
Lisa Jackson The Barrier Breaking Woman
Email: barrierbreakingwomen@gmail.com

For those of us who refuses to stay down, who even when we don't understand we keep going. The darkest moments of my life are why your listening, and that makes me the Sun rising in the midst of the darkness midnight. The words of A Barrier Breaking Woman.

HELP CONTACT LIST

Call 911

CHILDHELP NATIONAL CHILD ABUSE HOTLINE
www.childhelp.org
24/7

The National DOMESTIC VIOLENCE HOTLINE
www.thehotline.org
The National Domestic Violence Hotline
1-800-799-7233 or TTY 1-800-787-3224
24/7

RAINN The nations largest anti-sexual violence organization
www.rainn.org
Call 800.656.HOPE 4673

No Affiliation

The Sun Rises at Midnight

Here is a little journal just for you

Lisa Jackson

Notes

The Sun Rises at Midnight

Notes

Lisa Jackson

Notes

The Sun Rises at Midnight

Notes

Lisa Jackson

Notes

The Sun Rises at Midnight

Notes

Lisa Jackson

Notes

Notes

Lisa Jackson

Notes

Notes

Lisa Jackson

Notes

Notes